Lucille Lost

A TRUE ADVENTURE

VIKING

by Margaret George and
Christopher J. Murphy DVM, PhD

illustrated by
Debra Bandelin and Bob Dacey

To Cressida, companion of Troilus. And to Alison, their mistress.—M.G.

Dedicated to my daughters, Kaitlin and Savanna, who grew up surrounded by tortoises.—C.J.M.

To my mother, Sabra K. Harrington. —D.B.

VIKING
Published by Penguin Group
Penguin Young Readers Group, 345 Hudson Street, New York, New York 10014, U.S.A.

Penguin Books Ltd, Registered Offices: 80 Strand, London WC2R 0RL, England
First published in 2006 by Viking, a division of Penguin Young Readers Group

10 9 8 7 6 5 4 3 2 1

LIBRARY OF CONGRESS CATALOGING-IN-PUBLICATION DATA
George, Margaret,
Lucille lost / by Margaret George and Christopher J. Murphy ; illustrated by
Debra Bandelin and Bob Dacey.
p. cm.
Summary: Lucille, a pet Burmese tortoise, escapes from her home and ends up in the
woods, hoping to be rescued and returned to her family. Includes facts about tortoises.
ISBN 0-670-06093-3 (hardcover)
[1. Turtles—Fiction. 2. Lost and found possessions—Fiction.] I. Murphy, Christopher
John, date- II. Bandelin, Debra, ill. III. Dacey, Bob, ill. IV. Title.
PZ7.G293347Luc 2006
[E]—dc22   2005019632

Manufactured in China   Set in Kennerly   Book design by Jim Hoover

"Lucille! Tanky! You're going on an adventure!" Savanna Murphy said.

Savanna reached down, picked up Lucille, and offered her a tasty dandelion.

Boy, humans are warm, thought Lucille as she nestled in Savanna's lap. *And their bodies are so soft and squishy.*

"Mom and Dad said that while we're on vacation, you get to visit Troilus and his human family, the Georges. And when it's over we can tell each other about our adventures."

"Savanna! Where are you?" her mom called.

"Coming," she said, running out of the room.

———————

What's an adventure? Lucille asked Tanky.

Tanky looked down at Lucille. *It's when you go outside the pen and weird and wonderful things happen. Maybe you even get to see a bit of the world.*

I can't wait! said Lucille. *I want to go on an adventure and see the world.*

Be patient, Lucille! Adventure is waiting everywhere. You're only thirty years old, just a youngster.

Lucille brightened. Tanky was eighty-five years old and had a high-domed shell's worth of wisdom.

TORTOISE FACTS •

Lucille is a Burmese elongated tortoise. These tortoises can grow up to one foot long. They are called elongated tortoises because they have long, narrow shells. The domed part of the shell (the carapace) is yellowish-brown, with black "smudges." In the wild, Lucille's relatives live in moist forest areas.

Tanky is a California desert tortoise. They can grow up to fifteen inches long and weigh nine to fifteen pounds. They can live in the desert, where ground temperatures are greater than 140°F, because they spend most of their time in burrows where it's cooler. The number of desert tortoises in the wild has decreased by 90 percent in the past twenty years due to habitat loss, increased predation, and disease. It is now against the law to even touch a wild desert tortoise.

Soon it was time to take Lucille and Tanky over to Troilus and the George family.

"We've got your bags all packed," Kaitlin, Savanna's older sister, said to Tanky. Kaitlin loved Lucille, but Tanky was her favorite because he had been her grandmother's tortoise when her grandmother was a little girl.

Savanna picked up Lucille. "C'mon turtles, it's time to go visit Troilus."

"It's *tortoises*," said Kaitlin.

"I know, I know!" Savanna said. "Tortoises are turtles who live on land. I just said 'turtle' by mistake."

They put each tortoise in a box with a blanket lining. "Now they're ready to go."

TORTOISE FACTS ● ● ● ● ● ● ● ● ● ● ● ● ● ● ● ● ● ● ●
TORTOISE vs. TURTLE: Turtles and tortoises both belong to the scientific order *Chelonia*, the oldest living group of reptiles, dating back to the time of the earliest dinosaurs. Most turtles have flattened shells and webbed feet, and spend most of their time in water. Tortoises are a different type of turtle, which lives on land. They have high-domed shells and hind legs shaped like those of an elephant. They use water only to drink or bathe—they can't swim.

May my shell go soft if I'm not glad to see you two! said Troilus.

It's been too long, said Tanky. Lucille agreed.

Troilus's pen was fenced with railroad ties stacked up three high. It was full of healthy tortoise-food plants and shady bushes, perfect for dozing.

My house is over here, he said. *I think it's big enough for all of us.*

I don't know about that, said Tanky.

C'mon in, Tanky, said Lucille. She joined Troilus in his house.

CLUNK! The top of Tanky's shell hit the edge of the roof.

Then he lowered himself, inched in, stood up, and lifted the entire house off the ground on his shell.

Oh, no! cried Troilus.

Sorry, said Tanky as he set himself—and the house—back down. *I guess I'm not going to be able to sleep here.* They all walked out of the house.

Hmmm . . . I wonder. . . . Lucille eyed the flowers that hung over the edge of the pen.

What? said Troilus.

Have you been able to get any of those yummy-looking flowers?

No. They're too high for even Tanky to reach.

But maybe I can climb on Tanky's shell to get to them.

She gave it a try and returned to the ground with enough for everyone.

TORTOISE FACTS • • • • ·

Tortoise shells are soft when they first hatch from their eggs, and then they harden. Adults' shells can become soft if they eat the wrong kinds of food for a long time. The shell protects the tortoise from predators, such as raccoons, skunks, coyotes, and dogs. Native Americans used tortoise shells for bowls, spoons, and rattles, and the Chinese used ground-up shells in certain kinds of medicine. Tortoise shell is also made into jewelry, but it is illegal to bring this into the United States.

The next morning when Alison, the Georges' daughter, brought some fresh greens for Troilus and his guests, she couldn't find Lucille.

"Hello, Handsome! Where's Lucille?" she asked Tanky.

Alison looked all over the pen, but she didn't see Lucille anywhere.

Alison and her parents examined the walls of the pen, which were as sturdy—and tall—as ever.

They looked for paw prints, fearing that a dog or a raccoon might have snatched Lucille. But they found none.

Then they examined the yard like detectives, but still no trace of Lucille. Where had she gone?

The Georges asked their neighbors. No one had seen Lucille, but they joined the search.

"There's a treat for any kid who finds Lucille!" Mrs. George promised cheerily. But inside she was worried. There were so many places for a tortoise to hide. And if they didn't find Lucille by nightfall, she would have to tell the Murphys.

TORTOISE FACTS •

Even in a hurry, a tortoise can't get very far in a day. Its fastest burst of speed is only about 20 feet per minute, less than one tenth as fast as a human walking. But tortoises do move steadily and can cover a lot of ground. Aesop knew this when he wrote "The Tortoise and the Hare," where the tortoise wins the race against the hare because of its slow and steady movement to the finish line.

Meanwhile, Lucille was far away. Using a sleeping Tanky as her stepstool, she had gotten out of the pen at first light in search of adventure. The world seemed enormous—there was soft ground to walk on and a carpet of flowers to tempt her farther and farther from home.

Mmm . . . this is yummy! Lucille chewed a rose petal.

Just then, something warm lifted Lucille off the ground.

"What have we here?" said a smiling old man. He tipped her this way and that to make sure she wasn't hurt. "While I'm happy to have you dine at my garden table, I think it's best if I bring you back home."

That's fine, thought Lucille. *I can't wait to tell Tanky and Troilus about my adventure.*

"But where is your home? I'll just put you back in the woods down by Picnic Point, where a turtle like you will be very happy," said the man.

I'm a tortoise, not a turtle, thought Lucille. *And home is with Tanky and Troilus or back with the Murphys.*

But of course the man didn't understand anything she said.

Strapped to the back of a bicycle, Lucille watched the world stream by.

The man eventually stopped his bike at Picnic Point and carried her to a clearing in the woods near the shore of Lake Mendota, a large Wisconsin lake only a few blocks from Troilus's house.

"Maybe I should help you into the lake."

No . . . wait! Tortoises can't swim! Lucille screamed.

TORTOISE FACTS •
It's never a good idea to release an animal into the wild if it might be someone's pet.

"Or maybe you'll want to wander in by yourself," said the man. Then he put her on the grass and rode off, happy with the thought of a deed well done.

Lucille looked around at the strange woods and glittering blue lake. She turned and tried to take in her surroundings. There were tall trees, lots of weeds, wildflowers, and thick brush—so dense it looked like a wall. *How am I ever going to get home?* she wondered.

TORTOISE FACTS ●

Due to its slow metabolism, a tortoise can stay healthy for many days without eating. Wild tortoises can go for long periods without drinking, because they get water from the plants they eat. Tortoises kept as pets, however, should be fed every day and should always have fresh water available to drink.

For the next few hours Lucille walked in the woods, trails, and bike paths of Picnic Point. She got tired and hungry.

During those lonely hours Lucille met many different animals.

She asked each of them, *Where am I? And where can I find the Murphys?*

A skunk told her he didn't know what "the Murphys" meant.

They're warm and don't have shells, Lucille explained.

But I'm warm and I don't have a shell—is it me you are looking for? the skunk said.

A deer understood that she was looking for humans, but said, *You are better off being far away from them.*

A snake told Lucille to count her blessings—she was in the great hunting grounds, the very best place for catching mice.

As if I would want to catch a mouse, thought Lucille. *I just want to be back with Tanky and Troilus!*

TORTOISE FACTS ● ● ● ● · · · · · · · · · · · · · · · ·
Healthy tortoises have big appetites! Too much of any one thing (such as fruit) is not good for them. Grass, some flowers, and sprouts are excellent foods when added to a base diet of dark green leafy vegetables and vitamins. A calcium supplement will help to make their bones and shell strong. To keep them healthy, tortoises need sunshine and a shallow dish of fresh water for drinking and soaking.

That evening when Lucille still hadn't turned up, Mrs. George had to call the Murphys. She told them what happened, and what they had discovered. "A neighbor found Lucille and mistakenly let her go at Picnic Point."

Mrs. Murphy paused and said, "At least we know where to look. We'll come home tonight then, so we can join in the search."

The Great Tortoise Search was in full swing by the next day. LOST posters with Lucille's portrait were printed and tacked up on lampposts and trees throughout Picnic Point.

"I found her!" someone shouted.

Running toward Mr. Murphy was a little girl holding what seemed to be a squirmy Lucille. But as she came closer, something didn't seem right.

"Has Lucille lost weight?" asked Savanna.

Mr. Murphy frowned and turned the animal over. "You certainly have a fine . . . big . . . painted turtle here."

"You mean . . . this isn't Lucille?" The little girl was crushed.

"I'm afraid not," said Mr. Murphy. "This little guy is native to Picnic Point. You'd better take him back down to the marsh and let him go. And for us—it's back to the search."

TORTOISE FACTS •

Painted turtles look like an artist painted bright red and yellow markings on their black or greenish-brown shell. They are one of the most common turtles in North America and live in places with a lot of mud, like swampy areas, slow-moving streams, or the edge of lakes. They often are seen in small groups, sitting on logs or rocks as they soak up the sun's heat.

Lucille blinked her eyes several times. A big tortoise was standing in the shallow water by the edge of the shore. She started walking as fast as she could, shouting, *Tanky! Over here! How did you get here?*

Lucille stopped at the sand when she realized the big animal looming ahead wasn't Tanky. It was a snapping turtle!

Idonnashare, it said in a low growling voice, as it ripped off a piece of the fish it was eating.

TORTOISE FACTS ●

As its name suggests, the snapping turtle is a fierce predator. It feeds on fish and other small animals that live in or near water. They are best left alone, because they bite. Snapping turtles prefer quiet, muddy water, and spend most of their time submerged. The snapping turtle has a wormlike projection on its tongue that it wiggles like a fishing lure as it lies underwater, concealed in the mud.

I beg your pardon? Lucille squeaked.

I said, I . . . do . . . not . . . share. So keep out of my lake!

Lucille gasped. Legend had it that when a snapping turtle got hold of something in its powerful jaws, it wouldn't let go until the thunder rolled or the sun went down.

Rushing to get away from the lake's edge as fast as she could, Lucille realized she had climbed to the top of a strange mound in the forest. *Tanky! Troilus!* she wailed. *How will I ever get home now? I'm so lost!*

Home is where your shell is, said a crackly voice.

Who's there? Can you help me? pleaded Lucille.

Patience. Patience is what we're best at.

She looked up to see the oldest tortoise she had ever seen.

Patience? What are you talking about? Who are you? Where are you?

Hurry-Too-Fast was the way in, but Clear-Headed-Patience is the way out, said the Old Tortoise.

I don't understand.

Many lives ago, human friends of the land—and our clan—honored us with this turtle-shaped mound. The spirits of our ancestors and theirs hold power here. I have lived within the mound for countless seasons. I hear the spirits, and they tell me they will help you. He looked directly at Lucille and said in a clear strong voice, *Stop! Listen! Then act!* And with that, he disappeared.

TORTOISE FACTS • • • • • • • • • • • • • • • • • • •
Effigy mounds were built of earth over a thousand years ago by the native peoples of Wisconsin and nearby states. They are only about three feet high but can be over a hundred feet long. Effigy mounds are shaped to represent spirits and animals—birds, bears, panthers, and turtles, and are often found in areas near water, such as Picnic Point.

At the end of the second day of the Great Tortoise Search, Savanna asked sadly, "Do you think we'll ever find her?"

In a quiet voice, Kaitlin said, "I believe Lucille is safe. She knows we love her and miss her. She has to come back to us."

The girls watched as bats emerged into the night sky. A coyote howled off in the distance and an owl hooted far away.

"But it's scary out there," Savanna said. "Lucille could be hurt."

Kaitlin hugged Savanna, who reluctantly climbed into bed.

In the woods, Lucille could feel the air around her growing cooler. It was time to find a safe place where she could rest for the night. She located a tree root with a hollow space under it, withdrew into her shell, and slowly closed her eyes. As full darkness fell, the bats came out.

Only dimly aware of a howling coyote and hooting owl, Lucille fell asleep with the words of the Old Tortoise in her head.

TORTOISE FACTS ● ● ● ● ● ● ● ● ● ● ● ● ● ● ● ● ●

All reptiles, including tortoises, are cold blooded, meaning they must warm themselves up before they can hunt for food, digest, or perform other normal daily activities. Tortoises control their body temperature by absorbing the heat from the sun or a warm surface and by seeking shade in the hottest part of the day. At night, when the temperature drops, the tortoises' temperature also drops and they slow down. When the sun rises, the tortoises' temperature also rises, and they become active again.

As the sun warmed her the next morning, Lucille was filled with a new courage. She marched through the woods, determined to find a way home. Then she heard the Old Tortoise's voice loudly inside her head.

Stop! Lucille looked up and saw the most amazing thing. On the trunk of a tree was a tortoise. At first it didn't make any sense, for everyone knows tortoises can't fly. But as she walked closer she saw it wasn't a live tortoise but a picture—of her!

Listen! Two women came walking down a nearby path. One said to the other, "I hope someone finds that poor tortoise." But the women didn't recognize Lucille, who was in the woods, looking like a rock.

Act! Lucille placed herself smack in the middle of the trail and patiently waited to be found.

After several hours of being ignored, Lucille was finally spotted by a little boy.

"Mommy, Mommy, look what I found! Can I keep him?"

The little boy's mother had just finished reading a reward poster. She looked at the picture on the poster then walked over and studied Lucille.

"Noah, come here." She took him to look at the picture of Lucille. "It looks like your new friend is a *her* not a *him*, and she already has a home. Now we have to help her get back to it."

———————————

While the Georges had a party to celebrate Lucille's return, Lucille was telling Tanky and Troilus about her adventures.

And then I almost got put in a lake . . . and Tanky, I met the meanest turtle. A real snapping turtle! At first I thought it was you, 'cause it was sooo big! And then there was this old tortoise—even older than you, Tanky. . . . He spoke to me and then he vanished. She sighed. *Oh, it's so good to be back!*

Tanky and Troilus then told her about the Great Search.

Did you bring us back anything to eat? Troilus asked.

I'm sorry, the food wasn't that great. She looked up, remembering what started her adventure. *But I can climb on Tanky's back and get us some more flowers!*

TORTOISE FACTS ● ● ● ● ● ● ● ● ● ● ● ● ● ● ● ● ● ●

Tortoises can live a long time. Harriet, a giant Galapagos land tortoise who lives in Australia Zoo, Queensland, is over 175 years old! Many pet tortoises are passed down from parents to their children or grandchildren. Tanky was 80 years old when the Murphys began taking care of him.

While the adults talked inside, Kaitlin and Savanna went out to Troilus's pen to visit.

"I'm so glad Lucille is back," Kaitlin said.

"How do you think she got out?" Savanna asked.

"I guess we'll never know."